DEDICATION

This book is dedicated to my children Jasmin and Hari who have reminded me of the beauty and tranquility of Island life.

I hope this story encourages children to visit the Scottish Islands.

COPYRIGHT

All Rights Reserved © 2023 Ronalda Hira
All content, illustrations, and materials in this book are protected by copyright and intellectual property laws. The author and creator of this book is Ronalda Hira.

You may not modify, publish, transmit, participate in the transfer or sale of, reproduce, create derivative works from, distribute, perform, display, or in any way exploit any of the content, in whole or in part, without the express written permission of Ronalda Hira

This is Jasmin and Hari they live in London with their Mummy and Daddy.

Jasmin and Hari are going on holiday to see their Granny and Grandad, who live on a small island in Scotland.

The family arrives at the airport.

They help Daddy lift the heavy suitcases, and Hari asks, "When will we see our cases again?"

"When we get to Scotland," Jasmin excitedly replies.

They first must travel on a big plane. The pilot announces that they will land on time.

Jasmin and Hari scream in delight!

When Jasmin and Hari climb on board their second smaller plane, they giggle as their tall Daddy bumps his head.

"Ouch!" says Daddy.

Soon the small plane lands on the island and when they get off the plane, Jasmin and Hari can see Granny and Grandad waiting to welcome them.

They quickly start running towards them. They are all so happy to see each other!

On the car journey to Granny and Grandad's house, Jasmin says, "Look at all the lakes."

"In Scotland, we call them 'Lochs,'" Grandad tells Jasmin.

After unpacking, Mummy, Granny and Jasmin visit Jasmin's favourite café.

Jasmin eats delicious home-baked cookies.

Hari, Daddy and Grandad are feeding Grandads cows and sheep.

Hari watches as Grandad pours lots of food pellets for the sheep.

The sheep quickly gather around Hari and Grandad lets him help feed them.

As the sheep munch on the food pellets, Hari counts the sheep and shouts, "15!"

Hari watches Daddy and Grandad pick up a big bale of hay and put it in the field for the cows to chew.

That night, when Jasmin and Hari got into bed, they could hear a noise outside. They wonder what it could be.

Mummy explains that it is a bird called a Corncrake that is making the noise.

They fall asleep imagining what the Corncrake looks like.

Everyone has fun on the beach playing games, building sandcastles, and eating a delicious picnic.

The next day Jasmin and Hari are going on a Sea Tour with Mummy and Daddy.

Daddy, Jasmin and Hari visit the shop for treats for the day ahead.

Daddy takes lots of photos to show their friends back in London.

It is the last day of the holidays and Jasmin and Hari are sad to be leaving.

As they say goodbye to Granny and Grandad, Jasmin says, "I am going to cry forever."

Granny and Grandad say, "You know you can come back anytime."

They cheer and hug their Granny and Grandad.

Once they are on the plane Jasmin and Hari waved to Granny and Grandad until they were out of sight.

Jasmin and Hari are so happy and relaxed that they fall asleep on the plane, both dreaming of the best trip of their life.

1. How many planes did Jasmin and Hari fly on?

2. What did Jasmin eat at the café?

3. What animals did Grandad have?

4. What is the name of the bird Jasmin and Hari heard outside their window?

www.ingramcontent.com/pod-product-compliance
Lightning Source LLC
Chambersburg PA
CBHW041808070526
44585CB00026B/2884